HISTORY UNDERCOVER®

TOP SECRET

BY CAMERON BANKS

Look for these other

THE HISTORY CHANNEL.®

Titles:

THE HISTORY CHANNEL® PRESENTS
HAUNTED HISTORY™:
AMERICA'S MOST HAUNTED

THE HISTORY CHANNEL® PRESENTS
HISTORY'S MYSTERIES®: **BIZARRE BEINGS**

THE HISTORY CHANNEL® PRESENTS:
THE REAL SCORPION KING

THE HISTORY CHANNEL PRESENTS®

HISTORY UNDERCOVER®

TOP SECRET

BY CAMERON BANKS

SCHOLASTIC INC.
New York   Toronto   London   Auckland   Sydney
Mexico City   New Delhi   Hong Kong   Buenos Aires

No part of this publication may be reproduced in whole or in
part, stored in a retrieval system, or transmitted in any form or
by any means, electronic, mechanical, photocopying, recording,
or otherwise, without written permission of the publisher.
For information regarding permission, write to Scholastic Inc.,
Attention: Permissions Department,
557 Broadway, New York, NY 10012.

ISBN 0-439-53957-9

Copyright © 2003 A&E Television Networks.
The History Channel, the "H" logo, and HISTORY UNDERCOVER
are registered trademarks of A&E Television Networks.
All Rights Reserved.

Published by Scholastic Inc.

SCHOLASTIC and associated logos are trademarks and/or
registered trademarks of Scholastic Inc.

12 11 10 9 8 7 6 5 4 3 2 1   3 4 5 6 7/0

Printed in the U.S.A.

First printing, January 2003

Design by Louise Bova

Visit Scholastic.com for information
about our books and authors online!

CONTENTS

SHHHH!

Have you ever wondered what sorts of secrets lie inside folders that are marked STRICTLY CONFIDENTIAL? Or have you ever wanted to know more about forbidden experiments and daring, undercover missions? If so, then you've come to the right place: Step into our superprivate chamber, unlock the file drawers, and start learning all about history's most thrilling secrets!

Throughout time and across continents, extraordinary men and women have worked in the shadows of society, performing secret feats. Some were courageous heroes and leaders. Others were fearless explorers and innovators. But all worked quietly outside of the limelight, receiving little recognition for their efforts or achievements in their own time. . . .

In fact, some who have worked undercover were treated with suspicion — or worse! Risking their careers, reputations, and even their *lives* at times, the secret activities of a select few have changed the course of history.

From hidden tunnels to large cities, from the deepest depths of the ocean floor to the outer limits of our atmosphere, the reach of these incredible undercover "agents" has extended around the world . . . and beyond! Working with The History Channel®, we've tracked down the facts behind the stories that, for a long time, were kept under lock and key. And we're here to share all this amazing info with you . . . *if you can keep a secret!*

CONFIDENTIAL

1

UNDERCOVER HEROES

In the 1930s and 1940s, a few courageous men risked their lives by refusing to follow orders — and secretly saved *thousands* from certain death during World War II! Here are their incredibly heroic stories.

GERMANY, 1920s–1940

In the late 1920s, after World War I, Germany suffered economically. In 1933, a new leader named Adolf Hitler came to power, along with his Nazi political party. He promised social justice and a stronger Germany under his leadership. Hitler called his evil plan the "Final Solution," and it involved getting rid of all Jewish people and other "aliens" who lived in Germany.

By the 1930s, Hitler dreamed of taking over the world. With the conquest of Austria in March

1938, Hitler made his first major move toward creating a German-dominated Europe. Would he fulfill his evil goal? Not if some very heroic diplomats had their way!

THE EVIAN CONFERENCE

By 1938, many European Jews had realized that it was dangerous to remain in their own countries. But where could they go?

At the request of U.S. President Franklin Delano Roosevelt, representatives of thirty-two nations met in Evian, France, to work on the issue of refugees leaving Germany. But neither Great Britain nor the United States agreed to expand the number of foreigners they accepted each year.

The Evian Conference was considered a failure. The problems in Europe began to grow even *worse. . . .*

KRISTALLNACHT

Just months after the Evian Conference, a horrifying event showed that Hitler presented serious trouble. From November 9 to November 10, 1938, more than a thousand synagogues in Germany and Austria were burned. Seven thousand stores were looted, their windows smashed to pieces. But that was just the beginning of the horror of the government-authorized episode called *Kristallnacht*, "the night of broken glass." That night, thirty thousand Jewish boys and men were sent to concentration camps at Dachau, Buchenwald, and elsewhere in Germany.

WAR!

Soon after *Kristallnacht*, Germany attacked Poland, quickly taking control of the country. World War II officially began on September 3, 1939, six years after Hitler had assumed leadership of Germany.

By June 1940, Germany had invaded France and seized the capital city of Paris. The Germans decided to occupy northern France, leaving the southern half to be administered by a French "puppet regime" (known as the Vichy government) controlled by Germans.

More than a million refugees from the Netherlands, Austria, Germany, and Czechoslovakia fled to the south of France. Their hope was to get to neutral Spain or Portugal — or beyond. A lucky few found salvation in a man who risked *everything* to do what was right.

AN AMERICAN HERO IN MARSEILLES

By the summer of 1940, the situation in Europe was grave. Thousands of refugees fled to the large port city of Marseilles, France, seeking precious exit visas.

A visa is a document sometimes required for someone to leave a country and enter a new one. The office of the consulate of a country issues visas, and the consul general, vice-consul, and others are government officials who are responsible for issuing visas and other important official documents. In this role, these officials have

Brown Brothers

Hiram Bingham

much responsibility. They also have a great deal of potential power to help others in need.

In 1940, the Marseilles-stationed American vice-consul, Hiram "Harry" Bingham, had his career, courage, and values tested as *never* before. He would become one of the great heroes of the time!

MYSTERIOUS HEROISM

Artists, intellectuals, and scientists who opposed Nazis were part of a "Most Wanted" list created by Hitler. The German novelist Lion Feuchtwanger was on the list and was being held in a work camp in France in the summer of 1940. But a mysterious rescue mission saved Feuchtwanger's life.

One day, Feuchtwanger drifted away from his work team to a waiting car! Changing into women's clothing as a disguise, he was taken to Harry Bingham's villa in Marseilles, where he remained for six weeks before secretly moving to America. Exactly who arran-

CONFIDENTIAL FILES!

The German term *blitzkrieg* means "lightning attack." It entered the language when Germany's modern war machine of tanks and aircraft quickly destroyed Poland's large ground force!

ged Feuchtwanger's escape from the work camp remains a mystery to this day.

At that time, a young American journalist named Varian Fry volunteered to go to Marseilles

CONFIDENTIAL FILES!

Near the war's end, Fry wrote a book about his adventures in Marseilles. Harry Bingham was still in the foreign service and was mentioned only in passing. It's believed that Fry didn't want to endanger Bingham's career. But in Bingham's copy of the book, Fry wrote, *To Hiram Bingham, partner in the "crime" of saving human lives. . . . Varian Fry.*

for the Emergency Rescue Committee, a private American group. His secret mission was to find those on Hitler's "Most Wanted" list — and get them out of France. It was Varian Fry who enabled Feuchtwanger to go from Bingham's villa to the United States!

DANGEROUS DEALS

The consul general and other top officials told Harry Bingham not to get involved with trying to rescue the refugees in France. Bingham loved his job, and he knew that helping Jews escape was putting himself in

danger. But he had to do what he believed was right.

Faked and forged papers, bribes, and daring escapes were all part of the deadly game to rescue several thousand refugees. Harry Bingham risked everything to save the innocent. Years after Bingham's death, his son Bill discovered secret files about his father's heroic acts during World War II.

Bill Bingham explains, "I discovered my father had hidden files of photos and documents behind a fireplace in our colonial home. This was only a couple of years ago. When I opened them I was trembling. I was so excited. . . ." This was how Bill Bingham learned the amazing truth about his father.

Varian Fry's secret contacts with Bingham, the French underground, and others continued for a year. During that time, world-famous "enemies" of Hitler safely escaped to the United States. These included the artists Marc Chagall and Marcel Duchamp, the writer Franz Werfel, and Otto Meyerhof, a Nobel Laureate in Physiology, among many other people who made enormous contributions to society. Without the heroic acts of

Bingham and Fry, the world might have lost countless great individuals.

A MAN OF CONSCIENCE

Aristides de Sousa Mendes e Abranches was consul general of Portugal in Bordeaux, France. Although Portugal remained neutral throughout the war, its leader declared that Jews and other "enemies" of Germany were not welcome there. Knowing that thousands would face death, de Sousa Mendes could not turn his back on those in need!

A CHANCE MEETING

As consul general, de Sousa Mendes was responsible for handing out visas to foreigners who hoped to enter Portugal. By chance, he met Chaim Kruger, a rabbi from Poland. After hearing about the refugee's suffering, de Sousa Mendes offered him a visa!

Aristides de Sousa Mendes

Courtesy of Yad Vashem, The Holocaust Martyrs' and Heroes' Remembrance Auuthority, Jerusalem, Israel

However, the rabbi said he could not accept a visa unless other Jewish refugees received them as well. De Sousa Mendes was a devout Catholic and a good man, and he felt he had to do what was right.

In June 1940, de Sousa Mendes issued thirty thousand visas in three days. Within days, Jews and other refugees poured into Lisbon — the capital of Portugal — with visas signed by de Sousa Mendes. Immediately, the consul was called back to his own country, in serious trouble for disobeying orders!

THE HERO OF BAYONNE

On his way back to Lisbon, de Sousa Mendes found refugees crowding at the gates of the Portuguese consulate in Bayonne, France. Risking everything, he told a sub-consul, "If they were your family or your people, would you is-sue them visas? I or-der you to issue those visas."

De Sousa Mendes saved countless people that day. However, when he re-turned to Portugal, he was fired from the diplomatic corps after thirty years of faithful service! Unable to find work, he died in a charity ward.

?

TEST YOUR SECRET INTELLIGENCE!

With growing worries that Hitler would bomb London, 650,000 children were evacuated from the city and sent to the English countryside in 1939. True or false?

(Answer: True)

Decades later, de Sousa Mendes's heroism was finally recognized. The Portuguese government officially apologized to his family, awarding the ex-diplomat the Grand Cross of the Order of Christ, the country's highest civilian honor! He was also honored by Yad Vashem, the large memorial complex in Jerusalem, Israel, which recognizes those who risked their lives to save persecuted Jews.

CARL LUTZ AND THE INGENIOUS SCHUTZBRIEF

In 1942, Carl Lutz, a Swiss diplomat in Budapest, Hungary, courageously came up with an ingenious way to save Hungarian Jews, along with thousands of refugees from other countries!

TEST YOUR SECRET INTELLIGENCE!
Prior to joining the foreign service, Carl Lutz considered becoming a Methodist minister. True or false?

(Answer: True)

SAVING THE CHILDREN

Because Budapest was a safe haven for years, thousands of Jewish children from Poland and other countries had found foster homes with families there. But in 1942, all that changed. Certain the children would be sent to concentration camps,

Lutz worked to save them. Lutz told Hungarian officials that the neutral Swiss government would guarantee that the children would soon emigrate to Palestine (modern-day Israel). Then he pressured officials in Palestine to bend the rules to make room for the children. Because of Lutz's bold diplomacy, thousands of children reached a safe haven!

Carl Lutz

Courtesy of Agnes Hirschi

Carl Lutz succeeded in helping several thousand children. But his biggest challenge came two years later, when he worked to save *tens of thousands!*

CREATING SCHUTZBRIEF

On March 19, 1944, Germany invaded Hungary, overthrew the government, and began to work on destroying the country's Jewish population.

Carl Lutz knew he had to act fast to help the 200,000 Jews still in Budapest. If he could issue Swiss documents to Jews showing they were about to emigrate, then he could save them. He came up with a brilliant plan, inventing something called a *Schutzbrief* (which means, in German, "letter of protection.")

Lutz made a deal with German ruler Adolf Eichmann: Lutz could give away only eight thousand protective passes. But Lutz issued the passes several times over! He numbered the visas and gave them away — and when he got to eight thousand, he started all over again with a new set!

INTERNATIONAL HERO

After the war, Lutz's Swiss bosses discovered what Lutz had done and were not interested in his heroic deeds. They told Lutz that he had overstepped his authority.

But when the full nature of Carl Lutz's incredible courage came to light, this attitude changed. Lutz was recognized as an international hero for saving more than *62,000* refugees! During his lifetime, a street in Haifa, Israel, was named in his honor . . . and remains to this day!

DEFYING THE THIRD REICH

When Germany invaded neighboring Denmark in 1940, it promised the country's eight thousand

Jewish citizens would not be harmed. But by the summer of 1943, officials secretly called for the arrest of all Danish Jews. The bravery of a high-ranking German diplomat, defying the Third Reich (the Nazi empire) by acting on his own conscience, saved Denmark's entire Jewish population!

SPYING TO SAVE LIVES

Georg Ferdinand Duckwitz was Germany's shipping attaché in Denmark through the war. A man who loved Germany, not Hitler, Duckwitz dropped his membership in the Nazi party because he was disgusted by its racism. When he heard of the plan to round up Denmark's Jews, he wrote in his diary, "I knew what I had to do."

Risking more than his career, Duckwitz

CONFIDENTIAL FILES!

Why did the Nazis care what the Swiss thought — and why was Eichmann willing to let Lutz issue any visas at all? Because the Nazis were "laundering" hundreds of millions of stolen dollars through Switzerland, they wanted to maintain good relations with the country!

met secretly with the Swedish prime minister. Would neutral Sweden accept the Danish Jews?

Before he had an answer, Duckwitz secretly told key members of the Danish government about the plan to capture Jews that would happen in just a few days . . . unless they did something!

Sure enough, just before midnight on October 1, 1943, German storm troopers arrived to take away Jews. But *nobody* was home! The Danes had made sure that the Jews were safely evacuated.

TEST YOUR SECRET INTELLIGENCE!

By the summer of 1943, the Danish underground to fight against the Nazis had disappeared. True or false?

(Answer: False. The underground had grown and gotten stronger!)

INCREDIBLE COURAGE

Throughout the land, four million Danes aided their fellow Jewish countrymen. During the next three weeks, ninety percent of Denmark's Jews were evacuated and saved. Many spent the following two years in Sweden and returned safely to Denmark at the war's end.

At the time, few Danes knew about the tremendously courageous part Georg Duckwitz played in the great escape of 1943. If the German government had found out about his participation, they would have executed him immediately! Duckwitz's heroic spy work remained secret, and Duckwitz was able to work as a diplomat until Germany's surrender!

RIGHTEOUS AMONG NATIONS

Georg Duckwitz was the only member of the Third Reich's foreign service to receive Israel's highest honor, the Righteous Among Nations award. The award is for non-Jews who were responsible for saving a substantial number of Jewish lives. Only twenty-two diplomats have won the award.

After the war, Georg Duckwitz triumphantly returned to Denmark as the ambassador for a free Germany!

Millions survived World War II because of the bravery of diplomats such as Duckwitz, Bingham, de Sousa Mendes, and Lutz. Risking their jobs and their lives, these courageous "secret saviors" defied Hitler to do what was right. Their brave actions and legacy of courage will live on *forever*.

2

THE WORLD'S DEEPEST DIVE

In 1960, with little more than a tiny budget and a dream, a team of daring and innovative men secretly journeyed where no one had gone before . . . to the deepest depths of the ocean!

THE WORLD BENEATH THE SEA

What lies deep beneath the sea? If you traveled a good distance beneath the water you would discover huge mountain ranges and vast craters. But what about the *lowest* depth of the earth's oceans — the place in the western Pacific near Guam known as the Challenger Deep?

Traveling to the deepest point on Earth — nearly *seven miles* below the ocean's surface — became a burning mission for a team of brave explorers in 1960. The group encountered painful setbacks and real danger. Yet despite the challenges, they kept going and hit *real* rock bottom, breaking all records with the world's deepest dive!

PIONEERS OF THE DEEP

Human expeditions to discover the secrets hidden in the deep sea began in the early 1930s with explorers William Beebe and Otis Barton. Using a metal enclosure invented by Barton that was called a bathysphere, they descended 1,426 feet into the waters off the coast of Bermuda.

It took more than twenty years to push the world record just over 3,000 feet deeper. In 1952, Barton descended 4,700 feet in a dangling bathysphere. But the contraption's long cables were becoming dangerous at such extended depths.

The challenge? To create an independent, underwater craft that could take explorers deeper than ever!

THE AMAZING BATHYSCAPHE

Halfway around the world, a seventy-year-old

Swiss inventor named Auguste Piccard was at work creating a deep-sea vessel he called a bathyscaphe. In one early test run by the French Navy, the unmanned, empty bathyscaphe was sent deep into the ocean. The navy was horrified when it returned to the surface filled with water! But by 1953, the vessel successfully descended to a depth of 13,287 feet. For seven years, this record would remain unchallenged.

TEST YOUR SECRET INTELLIGENCE!

In Latin, the word *bathyscaphe* means "deep sea." True or false?

(Answer: False. It means "deep boat.")

THE TRIESTE

Auguste Piccard's next bathyscaphe was called the *Trieste* because it was built in Trieste, Italy. The *Trieste* was designed with life-support systems that provided oxygen and kept air pressure regular. The top part of the vessel was a float, with compartments filled with gasoline that was lighter than water. The bottom half of the craft was filled with more than four tons of releasable ballast, or weights, that provided the necessary weight to make a dive. Releasing ballast allowed the craft to then return to the surface.

With his son, Jacques, Piccard used the ingeniously designed *Trieste* for a deep dive in 1955, reaching a maximum depth of 10,390 feet! The Piccards were among the first people *ever* to witness some of the awesome wildlife of the deep sea.

CONFIDENTIAL FILES!

Did you know that although sunlight does not reach the depths of the ocean, light is actually produced there? Scientists have found that ninety percent of deep-sea creatures are bioluminous, which means they make light of their own! That glowing light helps the creatures attract mates, avoid predators, and find food.

But it was very expensive to run the *Trieste,* and by 1956 the Piccards sought to lease or sell the craft. After observing and participating in several test dives, the U.S. Office of Naval Research bought the *Trieste* bathyscaphe in 1958 for $250,000 (which is equivalent to about one million dollars today) and shipped it to San Diego. A whole new era of deep-sea exploration was about to begin.

PROJECT NEKTON

The word *nekton* means (in German) a group of creatures able to swim independently. Under U.S. Navy oceanographer Andy Rechnitzer, the program director of the bathyscaphe project, the *Trieste*'s quest for deeper depths got a code name: Project Nekton.

With submarine officer Lieutenant Don Walsh as the officer in charge, Lieutenant Larry Shumaker leading the engineering on the bathyscaphe, and Jacques Piccard working as a technical consultant, the team was ready to explore just how low the *Trieste* could go!

LATE NIGHTS

Although Jacques Piccard was hired by the navy to teach the team how to "drive" the *Trieste*, team members believed they could learn only by doing it themselves — without Piccard! After Piccard would leave for the day, the other men would stay on, working until eleven-thirty every night.

While the navy funded the project, the Nekton team operated independently. But once the team had mastered the bathyscaphe, they knew they were ready for the next challenge, which would only happen with approval from the highest ranks of the navy. In 1959, Admiral Aleigh Burke, the senior admiral in the navy, gave the go-ahead for a mission never before attempted: to journey to the bottom of the ocean!

CREATING TECHNOLOGY

There was just one problem: How could you go down 36,000 feet in a vessel that had never traveled even close to that distance? The team realized that the pressure on the *Trieste* at that depth would be enormous and that they would have to modify the craft before attempting a dive anywhere *near* that deep.

To withstand a deeper dive, the *Trieste* needed a larger float, or hull, and ballast containers. The new sphere, which weighed thirteen tons and had the capacity to hold sixteen tons of ballast, took six months and cost $65,000 to make ($65,000 in the 1950s is equivalent to about half a million dollars today). The refurbished vessel was designed to withstand pressure down to 40,000 feet, but there was no way to be certain.

For the ultimate test, Project Nekton moved its

operations to Guam, home of the deepest waters in the world!

TEST DIVE

In November 1959, the Project Nekton team loaded sixteen tons of ballast and pumped 33,000 gallons of gasoline into the vessel in preparation for a deep test dive in the warm waters of the South Pacific. It would prove to be a *most* challenging time.

UNEXPECTED EXTREMES

When oceanographer Andy Rechnitzer and pilot Jacques Piccard began their descent, the temperature inside the bathyscaphe was about ninety degrees Fahrenheit, with extremely high humidity. The two began perspiring heavily and felt sick as they began to go deep under the surface.

But when they traveled just 500 feet down, the *Trieste* began to cool off. (It was thirty-seven degrees Fahrenheit outside the craft and just a little warmer within!)

CONFIDENTIAL FILES!

Around the world, the ocean is about two miles deep, on average. But at the deepest part of the ocean at the Challenger Deep of the Mariana Trench off the coast of Guam, vast gashes in the bottom make the ocean more than 35,000 feet — or nearly seven miles — deep. If you dropped Mount Everest into the Challenger Deep, its peak would be more than a mile below the surface of the water!

And by the time they reached their target of 18,150 feet — a new record — the men were freezing! Nevertheless, the three-hour journey was a success.

But when they reached the surface, Rechnitzer and Piccard heard a loud explosion coming from the *Trieste* — a possible catastrophe for Project Nekton!

RACE AGAINST TIME

Though the men were unharmed by the explosion, the *Trieste* was badly affected. When the team examined the bathyscaphe, they found several gallons of water had leaked in. And the team had only two more months until the weather in Guam would no longer allow them to start on their mission. The team needed to repair the vessel immediately, but replacing the hull with a new one could take more than eight months. Any longer delay would make the navy cancel the project.

Suddenly, the race against time was on! Discovering that rapid changes in water temperature had caused the hull to crack, the desperate team came up with a novel solution: realigning the sphere with a huge battering ram made out of a forklift and using gasket sealant from a local auto parts store to seal its joints.

By January 1960, the team had tested the repaired *Trieste* at depths down to 1,000 feet. But it was nearly typhoon season, and the weather was getting bad. The Project Nekton team had to make a decision: Risk diving to the bottom then, or return home defeated!

DANGEROUS CONDITIONS

Finally, the team reached a decision: They would make the dive! The chief of naval operations declared that Jacques Piccard and Lieutenant Don Walsh would pilot the mission.

On January 23, 1960, the day of

the dive, navy support ships were stationed 250 miles off the coast of Guam. But as minutes passed, weather and sea conditions deteriorated rapidly. Just as the team decided the *Trieste* was ready to go, a message came from the U.S. Navy Electronics Laboratory.

The message? *"Cancel dive!"*

SECRET DESCENT!

With the *Trieste* on the surface waiting to go, there was still time to stop the dive. But Andy Rechnitzer decided to pretend that the *Trieste* had already begun its descent before it received the message from the electronics

CONFIDENTIAL FILES!

At the smooth, barren bottom of the ocean, Walsh and Piccard discovered that there was no water current.

laboratory. He sent a message to the navy that the vessel was already 20,000 feet underwater and gave the Project Nekton team the go-ahead, giving the team and its ship a chance to make history!

As Walsh and Piccard went down deeper, and the temperature cooled and pressure increased, the walls of the cabin began to shrink inward. At

20,000 feet below the surface of the ocean, water began to leak in! Would they survive?

But soon the outside pressure pushed the walls outward again, sealing the leaks. The *Trieste* kept diving. . . .

NO POINT OF RESCUE

Both Walsh and Piccard knew that if the bathyscaphe broke in any way at their advanced depth, it would mean a watery death! Communication with the Project Nekton team on the surface was difficult and unpredictable. All they could do was hope and pray that the mission would go as planned.

TEST YOUR SECRET INTELLIGENCE!

The water pressure is so great at the bottom of the ocean that a leak in the cabin of a bathyscaphe could become a dangerous water jet whose stream could actually cut a person. True or false?

(Answer: True)

At 30,000 feet, Walsh and Piccard were shocked by an explosion that jolted the sphere! All systems seemed to be working, so they chose to accept the possible risk and continue their descent.

Finally, at more than 37,000 feet — deeper than expected — the divers began to get a trace of the ocean floor on their instruments. Their tense five-and-a-half-hour journey ended as they settled on the ocean floor. With little expectation that they would be heard, the two explorers reported their depth to the topside crew — who miraculously heard the message!

ROCK BOTTOM

From more than seven miles below the surface of the water, Jacques Piccard peered out a small porthole and reported seeing flat fish, a shrimp, and a jellyfish. Turning on a light, the pair discovered that a back window had cracked, causing the earlier explosion. Although it wasn't a problem then, they didn't know if it would cause a pressure problem when they resurfaced, possibly sealing the pair inside!

At 6,300 fathoms — about 37,800 feet — deep, the explorers repaired the window and began collecting scientific data. After sitting in water that was slightly above freezing temperatures for twenty minutes, they dropped 800 pounds of ballast and began the trip back to the water's surface.

VICTORY!

At 4:56 P.M., nine and a half hours after they began their mission, Walsh and Piccard broke the sur-

CONFIDENTIAL FILES!

In 1963, when the U.S.S. *Thresher* nuclear submarine sank in the Atlantic Ocean, the navy brought in the *Trieste* to successfully locate the crash site and recover remains from the vessel. The *Trieste* is now on display at the Naval Museum in Washington, D.C.

face of the Pacific. As they pumped air into the exit chamber to clear it, the cracked window remained airtight. Fifteen minutes later they unlatched the 400-pound door — and stepped into the afternoon sunshine!

Photographers from *National Geographic* and *Life* magazines were there to record the historic event. Once aboard the U.S.S. *Lewis*, the explorers took an American flag, encased in a Plexiglas frame, and sent it down to the spot where they had landed on the ocean floor! Later, the entire Nekton team flew to Washington, D.C., and received special merit awards from President Dwight D. Eisenhower.

While many people have traveled into space or climbed Mount Everest, to this day, only two people have journeyed to the deepest part of the ocean. The mission was accomplished through the heroic efforts of a team who bravely set out into the unknown . . . and came back alive to tell of its wonders!

3
SECRET ASTRONAUTS

When American men first went into space in the 1960s, millions watched in awe. What few knew then was that thirteen *women had* also qualified to become astronauts! Since women were not allowed to be astronauts, they were secretly trained. These thirteen amazing women, called the Mercury Thirteen, had the "right stuff," but were the wrong gender. Read on to find out how they went against the rules . . . but finally got their way!

PIONEERS OF THE AIR

In the earliest days of air travel, flying a plane was a job for men only. But in 1910, a New York journalist named Harriet Quimby became the first woman to earn a pilot's license in the United States. In April 1912 she became the first woman to fly across the English Channel!

Harriet Quimby forged the way for other women to fly. Since being a pilot was a requirement for becoming an astronaut, Quimby's achievement helped women to eventually travel through the atmosphere! But even when they qualified to become astronauts, women who dared to *soar* were unable to pursue their dream . . . simply because they were women!

FLYING FLAPPERS

By the 1920s, women had gained important freedoms, such as the right to vote. At that time, the number of female pilots grew. But instead of being taken seriously by the rest of the world, women  pilots were called "Flying Flappers." Flappers was the term given to fun-loving girls of the 1920s. Female flyers were also called "Petticoat Pilots," named after underclothes for women! Although the women pilots were full professionals, their flight show performances were not presented as real feats.

In fact, in the 1920s, the International Aeronautical Federation (a group that certified speed and altitude records) didn't even *mention* any records of female pilots! Instead they noted the achievement of women as merely "miscellaneous air performances."

But the early female pilots were more than attractions at air shows. Actually, these women were some of the first test pilots, proving how high and fast aircrafts could go!

THE "NINETY-NINES"

In 1929, the International Aeronautical Federation *finally* recognized the record-breaking flights of women. On August 14, female pilots gathered to hold the first Women's Air Derby. The tough eight-day race — which the press called the "Powder Puff Derby" — ran from California to Ohio.

The female flyers who met at the derby decided to create an association. Since ninety-nine of the 126 licensed women pilots pledged their support, the group

?

TEST YOUR SECRET INTELLIGENCE!

Harriet Quimby's flight across the English Channel might have gotten more attention had it not been for the fact that the day after her flight, the *Titanic* sank! True or false?

(Answer: True)

called itself the Ninety-nines. They elected thirty-two-year-old air ace Amelia Earhart president.

Earhart encouraged other women to work toward the dream of becoming a pilot, despite all obstacles. Pilot Jacqueline Cochran took her advice. Over time, she would become a driving force for women who reached for the stars . . . literally!

WOMEN PILOTS AND THE WAR EFFORT

In 1940, Jackie Cochran set a new speed record of 332 miles per hour. That was faster than any woman *or man* had ever flown before! When America entered World War II in 1941, Cochran believed women pilots could serve their country.

She approached General Hap Arnold, the commanding general of the Army Air Forces, about starting a women's air corps. General Arnold liked the idea, and in 1943 created the Women's Air Force Service Pilots — or WASP — program. Jackie Cochran became a director of WASP.

?

TEST YOUR SECRET INTELLIGENCE!

In May 1932, Amelia Earhart became the first woman to fly over the Atlantic Ocean on her own and the only person to fly it twice. She also made the crossing in record time. True or false?

(Answer: True)

Twenty-five thousand women applied for just a thousand WASP pilot positions! Once they completed tough training, the women pilots risked their lives right alongside men. In fact, during the war, thirty-eight of these pilots died in flying accidents!

CONFIDENTIAL FILES!

Decades after WASPs died in the war, investigations revealed that some of the women died as a result of sabotage. Just who tampered with their planes remains uncertain!

MEN, WOMEN, AND THE SPACE RACE!

After the war, Jackie Cochran continued to prove women pilots could do just as well as men. In 1953, she flew a jet fighter 653 miles per hour, becoming the first woman to break the sound barrier!

In the meantime, the Soviet Union (or the U.S.S.R.) was hard at work on going even faster — and farther — into space. By 1957, Soviets sent the *Sputnik* satellite into the atmosphere. It was the first time a man-made object had been launched into space.

The space race had begun, and the United States needed to catch up! In 1959, the new National

Aeronautics and Space Administration (NASA) announced plans to put the first man into space. Jackie Cochran had a plan, too — a plan that included *women* in the race against the Russians!

PROJECT MERCURY: SEARCH FOR SUPER PILOTS.

Project Mercury was America's first manned space program. In 1959, as engineers assembled a rocket, NASA searched for super pilots to fly it! Thirty-two of the country's top test pilots were chosen to take tests to see if they had the "right stuff."

Dr. Randy Lovelace, director of the Lovelace Clinic, conducted many tests on the candidates — all men — to determine how they would react to the stresses of space flight. The candidates were pushed to the limits of their endurance — and then pushed again.

Finally, in April 1959, NASA announced that seven male pilots were selected for the Mercury

CONFIDENTIAL FILES!

Breaking the sound barrier means going faster than the speed of sound. On October 14, 1947, Chuck Yeager became the first pilot to break the sound barrier.

program. Known as the Mercury Seven, this elite group of men would set a superior standard for astronauts — which, later, would be tested by women.

THE INCREDIBLE JERRIE COBB

In September 1959, Dr. Lovelace attended an international medical meeting in Moscow. There, he heard that the Russians were considering putting a woman in space. Dr. Lovelace and his colleagues decided to put a woman through the same tests as the Mercury Seven.

A twenty-eight-year-old pilot named Jerrie Cobb seemed like the perfect candidate for an American female astronaut. She had been flying since she was twelve years old and had set world speed records!

In February 1960, Cobb reported to the Lovelace Clinic for exams testing her physical, intellectual, and emotional endurance. She did very well on more than seventy-five difficult tests! In some cases, she did better than the men Dr. Lovelace had tested.

MORE FLYING FEMALES?

Jerrie Cobb did *so* well on the tests that Dr. Lovelace declared she was ready for space! In September 1960, she took more endurance tests and did extremely well — *again*. But would other women do as well as Cobb?

Dr. Lovelace decided to test other women to find out how they would react to space flight. He asked Jackie Cochran to help find qualified candidates. A select group of those women would become a secret part of the space program. . . .

THE SEARCH FOR THE MERCURY THIRTEEN

Like the male astronauts of the Mercury Seven, Jerrie Cobb demonstrated amazing physical toughness and had great technical skills. The

search was now on for other women pilots who had the right stuff to become an elite group called the Mercury Thirteen (after the Mercury Seven).

In the summer of 1961, twenty women took the incredibly difficult astronaut tests at Lovelace Clinic — and twelve passed. In the meantime, Jerrie Cobb was taking still more tests. She passed them with flying colors!

The Russians had put the first *man* into space

CONFIDENTIAL FILES!

The women at Lovelace Clinic took the same exams that male astronauts such as Alan Shepard and John Glenn had taken. These included a vertigo test, which measured how *airsick* a pilot would get. If you don't like roller-coaster rides, you probably wouldn't be a great candidate for an astronaut!

just a few months earlier. Now Jerrie Cobb suggested a radical idea: An American *woman* could be the first woman in space!

FIGHTING TO FLY

Just one step was left for the Mercury Thirteen before they were ready to soar. The women needed to have experience flying jets. The Pensacola Naval Air Station in Florida agreed to give the women special jet orientation training. But two days before training was to start, the navy suddenly withdrew its support of the program. The plan for women to go into space was canceled!

Jerrie Cobb and other female fliers didn't want to take no for an answer. They were determined to fight for the right of women to go into space for their country!

APPEALING TO CONGRESS

Jane Hart, one of the Mercury Thirteen astronaut trainees, was married to Michigan Senator Philip Hart. In 1962, Hart convinced Congress to hold hearings on whether the women astronauts had faced discrimination. Cobb explained that women were blocked from becoming astronauts because they did not have jet pilot training the way men did.

Astronaut John Glenn argued against the women. He said, "The fact that women are not in this field is a fact of our social order." Was America — and the world — simply not ready for female astronauts?

Incredibly, Jackie Cochran didn't support the female astronauts, either! Although she was out of town at the time of the hearings, she sent in testimony stating, "I am as eager as the next [woman] to go into space. Yet I know : . . that is not in the national interest." The women of the Mercury Thirteen felt stunned — and betrayed!

?

TEST YOUR SECRET INTELLIGENCE!

In 1963, a Russian textile worker became the first woman in space, spending three days in orbit. True or false?

(Answer: True. Her name was Valentina Tereshkova.)

A LOSING BATTLE

Jackie Cochran had funded many of the tests for the female astronauts. She had led the WASPs during World War II. Why would she testify against a space program for women astronauts?

Many believe that Cochran realized the fight for women to go into space was a losing battle. The time and place were wrong, and she accepted that.

Still, the thirteen women lost their chance to become astronauts. It was bitterly disappointing. And it would take another *twenty years* before an American woman ventured into space.

WOMEN IN SPACE . . . FINALLY!

While the Mercury Thirteen never made it into space, the contributions of these women live on.

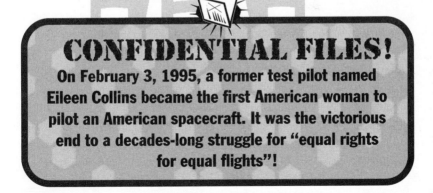

CONFIDENTIAL FILES!

On February 3, 1995, a former test pilot named Eileen Collins became the first American woman to pilot an American spacecraft. It was the victorious end to a decades-long struggle for "equal rights for equal flights"!

Their daring careers as pilots and their performance tests in the space program paved the way for other women — and for all astronauts.

On June 18, 1983, Dr. Sally Ride became the first American woman to fly in space. It was a historic moment for women everywhere. In October 1984, Kathy Sullivan became the first American woman to walk in space. To date, more than twenty-five American female astronauts have flown among the stars!

CONFIDENTIAL FILES!

You can find out more about NASA and women in space exploration at *http://www.nasa.gov/women/welcome.html*

Astronaut Pam Melroy believes that the secret tests of the Mercury Thirteen were incredibly important. "We enjoy a level of credibility, of respect and acceptance, that we would not have but for those women," she says. "And they fought every inch of the road ahead of us to enable us to enjoy what we have now."

From Harriet Quimby's first flight in 1910, women pilots worked hard — sometimes *secretly* — to win equality in the skies. It has been a quest that inspired dreams, conquered fears, created adventures . . . and made history!

THE HISTORY CHANNEL

Join us as we peek inside some of history's most confidential files to investigate several seriously secretive cases....

CONFIDENTIAL

THE HISTORY CHANNEL

This is the Garden of the Righteous Among Nations in the Yad Vashem memorial in Jerusalem, Israel. Yad Vashem honored Aristides de Sousa Mendes, and other amazingly brave heroes, for saving thousands of lives during the Holocaust.

AP/Wide World Photos

THE HISTORY CHANNEL.

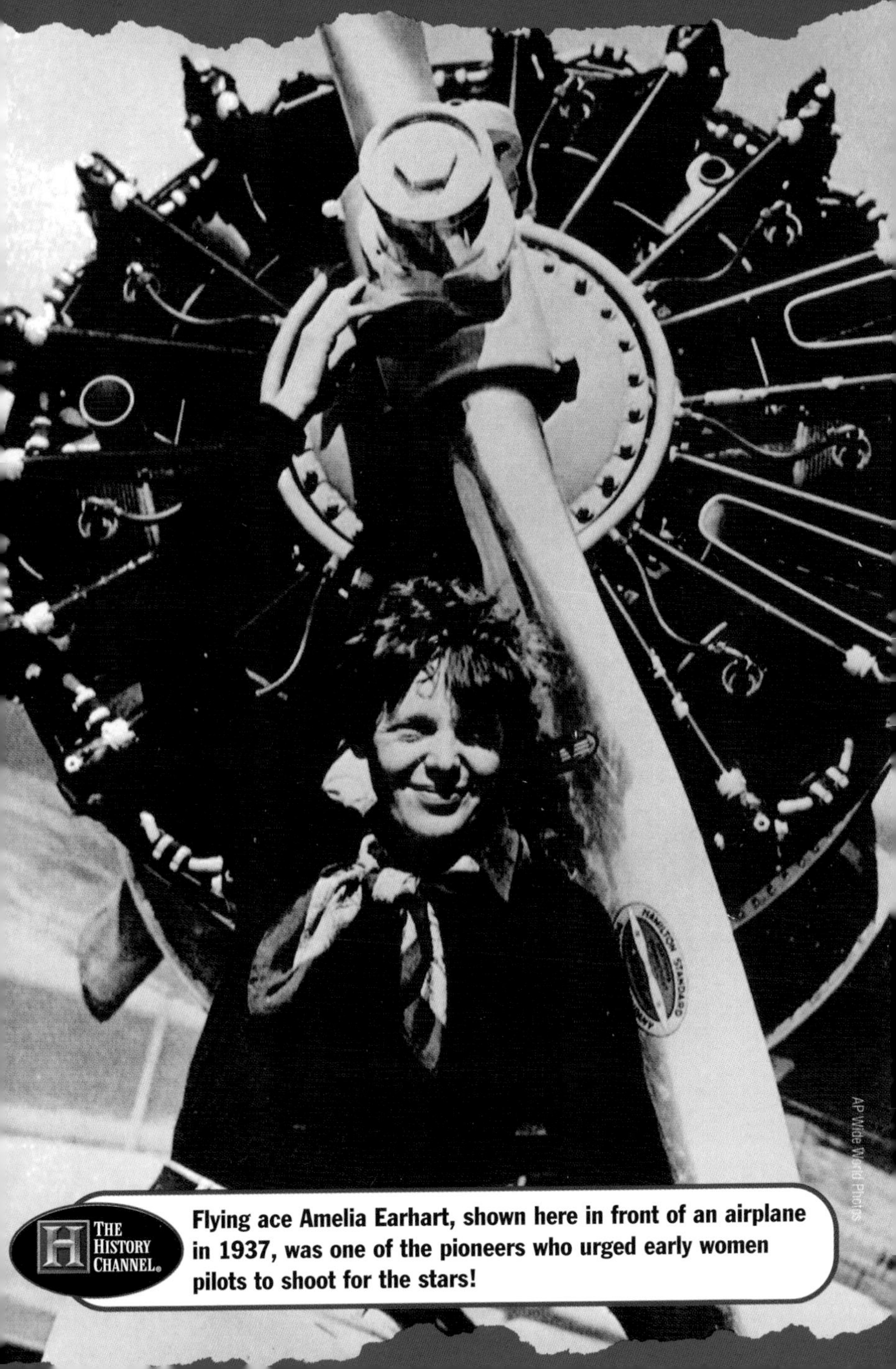

Flying ace Amelia Earhart, shown here in front of an airplane in 1937, was one of the pioneers who urged early women pilots to shoot for the stars!

In 1983, astronaut Sally Ride became the first American woman in space. It was thanks to the bold acts of the Mercury Thirteen that women like Sally Ride were able to make it all the way into space.

This is the space shuttle *Discovery*, achieving liftoff on March 8, 2001, at the Kennedy Space Center in Cape Canaveral, Florida. The daring undercover actions of the Project Manhigh astronauts made possible the advanced space travel of today.

THE HISTORY CHANNEL

Auguste Piccard's amazing bathyscaphe, the *Trieste*, was equipped to take people deeper into the ocean than they had ever gone before. Here it is shown after a deep dive in 1953.

The Cold War between the United States and the Soviet Union involved a lot of secret espionage activity. . . some of which was all done through the mind!

These are the CIA (Central Intelligence Agency) headquarters outside of Washington, D.C. During the Cold War, the CIA made top secret use of a few incredible psychic spies!

4

SNEAKING INTO SPACE

While women worked undercover to become astronauts, another daring group of pioneers was secretly entering the outer limits of our atmosphere. With incredible courage and determination, a remarkable American team of "pre-astronauts" became the first to explore secrets at the edge of space.

DREAMS OF SPACE

In the 1950s, the only people flying in space were comic book heroes. Few people took the subject seriously, or actually believed that humans were ever going to be able to go into space. But a brilliant team at Holloman Air Force Base in New Mexico persisted in achieving the dream of space travel.

With very little money or support but plenty of courage and optimism, these pre-astronauts proved the impossible. For the first time in history, humans traveled to the edge of space!

HOW FAST CAN THEY GO?

In 1946, Dr. John Paul Stapp was a young air force medical doctor. As rocket-fueled travel began to develop, Dr. Stapp explored an important question: How fast could a person go and still be safe?

A G force is the force of gravity during acceleration (speeding up) and deceleration (slowing down). Until Dr. Stapp began experiments in the early 1950s, the air force believed that humans could only endure eighteen G forces, or eighteen times the force of normal gravity.

Using himself as a guinea pig in experiments with different levels of gravity, Dr. Stapp found human endurance was a lot greater than that. The doctor found that humans could withstand double — or even triple — the limit of eighteen G forces! This revolutionary research kicked off a program that would test the outer limits of human endurance.

ANIMALS IN SPACE

At the time of Dr. Stapp's investigations, very

little was known about Earth's upper atmosphere. The air force began sending up animals (such as dogs and apes) in the nose cones of rockets to determine the effects of space on living tissue. You could even say that the very *first* astronauts walked on four legs! Early experiments tested both real and imagined threats of space flight on living beings. Research with mice proved that the creatures could survive a trip into the atmosphere.

The next step? For Stapp, by then an air force colonel, the challenge was clear: to work on sending men where only mice had gone before!

?

TEST YOUR SECRET INTELLIGENCE!

True space begins one hundred miles above Earth. True or false?

(Answer: false. Space begins sixty-two miles above Earth.)

UP IN THE ATMOSPHERE

Major David Simons, an aeromedical

doctor, had become an expert in supervising animal flights. In 1955, Colonel Stapp asked him if he would like to take a ride up in a capsule *himself*! Major Simons said yes, and an amazing experiment called Project Manhigh was born.

BIG BALLOONS

In the mid-1950s, rockets didn't have the power to launch heavy loads into the stratosphere. To send Simons into space, Project Manhigh used a balloon — a huge helium balloon! Suspended beneath the balloon in a capsule, Simons would ride 100,000 feet — about twenty miles — to the threshold of outer space!

A balloon engineering company, Winzen Research, created the capsule — or gondola — that carried Simons. Seven feet high and three feet wide, it was no larger than a closet! But it had all the systems to keep a man alive in space, from a primitive air-conditioning system to a mixed-gas atmosphere.

TEST RUN

Before Simons went into space, Colonel Stapp decided that Project Manhigh needed a short test flight, which he called Manhigh I. To fly it, he chose Captain Joe Kittinger, a test pilot with nerves of steel. Kittinger and Simons trained rigorously.

On June 2, 1957, conditions at Fleming Field in Minnesota were excellent for flying. Although takeoff of the 180-foot-tall balloon went perfectly, the team soon discovered that Joe Kittinger's radio transmitter had broken! And that was just the *start* of trouble. . . .

NO TIME FOR JOKES!

As Kittinger rose to a record-breaking 96,000 feet, the ground crew began to panic. The capsule was losing oxygen fast. Somehow the oxygen sys-

CONFIDENTIAL FILES!

In Manhigh's pressurized capsule, the risk of fire was *immense*. Since oxygen is highly flammable, Manhigh engineers rejected using one hundred percent oxygen for the pilot to breathe. Instead, they used a mixture of sixty percent oxygen, twenty percent nitrogen, and twenty percent helium — which made the pilot's voice as high-pitched and squeaky as a cartoon character's!

tem had been installed in reverse, and Kittinger was in grave danger!

Kittinger had barely enough oxygen to return to Earth. The crew told him to come down immediately. His reply? "Come and get me!" Was Kittinger's judgment already affected by the loss of oxygen?

Actually, Kittinger was joking and had already started the difficult process of valving gas to come back down. He landed nine hours after launch, dangerously low on oxygen. Other than the oxygen valve error, the flight was considered a success.

MANHIGH II

No one before had ever tried to spend a full day and night in space. But in August 1957, Simons was ready! There were several dangers Simons knew he was facing. Since he was going twenty miles above the earth, Simons would be above ninety-nine percent of the earth's atmosphere and surrounded by temperatures of minus one hundred degrees Fahrenheit. That's pretty chilly!

Still, Simons and the crew went ahead with the mission. The crew freed the balloon and Simons rose to a record-breaking altitude of 101,500 feet above the earth.

As he rose into the atmosphere, Simons became the first person to see the shape of the earth below. He also took the first photos from the edge of space!

DINNERTIME

All was going well for the Manhigh II mission. But crew members noticed that Simons was beginning to sound groggy. When he was questioned, the team realized that Simons had forgotten to eat anything in twelve hours!

Simons's menu for the flight included standard air force rations — a hamburger and a candy bar. After he ate something, Simons cheered up and felt more awake.

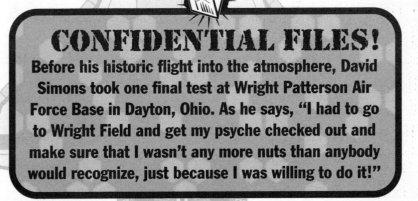

CONFIDENTIAL FILES!

Before his historic flight into the atmosphere, David Simons took one final test at Wright Patterson Air Force Base in Dayton, Ohio. As he says, "I had to go to Wright Field and get my psyche checked out and make sure that I wasn't any more nuts than anybody would recognize, just because I was willing to do it!"

STORMY WEATHER

It was a good thing that Simons became more alert. He soon realized his altitude was dropping, and the balloon was heading straight for a thunderstorm! Colder air could make the balloon brittle, and turbulence from the storm was enough to destroy the vessel — and Simons. The resourceful Simons dropped in some reserve power batteries and gained 5,000 feet.

Once he was out of danger, Simons said he was delighted to see the sun rise, knowing it would warm the balloon!

The next morning, crew members noticed that the pilot's speech was slurred because his carbon dioxide levels were dangerously high. But Simons soon landed in a farmer's field in South Dakota. As the first man who had survived twenty-

TEST YOUR SECRET INTELLIGENCE!

During his historic, 24-hour flight to the edge of space, David Simons lost five pounds! True or false?

(Answer: False. He lost a whopping seventeen pounds!)

four hours on the edge of space, he had made history!

SPACE RACE!

Although Manhigh II was a success, the program had run out of money. In fact, Colonel Stapp and Major Simons couldn't even afford a tiny staff to analyze data from the flight. But soon, an incredible international event suddenly changed *everything*.

In the fall of 1957, the Soviet Union launched *Sputnik*, the world's first satellite — and the space race was officially on! Suddenly, funds were available for another flight for the Manhigh team.

A PERFECT SPACE TRAVELER?

Manhigh III's goal was to identify and select the perfect space traveler. Data from the flight would be used for the Mercury program at the newly created NASA.

The role of the pilot in Manhigh III would be different from other flights. Instead of giving the capsule pilot complete control, a panel of on-ground experts would make all important decisions. Now the pilot would be the "body" and the panel of experts, the "brain"!

Twenty-six-year-old Lieutenant Clifton McClure was selected for the flight. A brilliant engineer, amazing test pilot, and amateur astronomer, he seemed the perfect candidate to enter space!

LIFE OR DEATH

The first two attempts to launch Manhigh III in October 1958 were canceled due to bad weather. But finally, McClure got his chance to head into the stratosphere! On October 8, at ten A.M., he had reached peak altitude of 99,700 feet!

But somehow, his capsule's dry ice cap (which was used to cool the capsule) was missing! The temperature was rising rapidly inside the capsule, and McClure's own temperature was already 102 degrees. His temperature continued to rise to *106* as the capsule baked, creating a life-or-death situation!

To make matters worse, just after McClure was ordered to come down, his radio suddenly failed! Amazingly, the pilot navigated a brutal descent over the San Andreas Mountains where, incredibly, when crew members discovered McClure he was not only alive — but smiling!

LESSONS LEARNED

The overheating of the Manhigh III capsule taught the team that effective cooling was vitally important. They also learned that humans could survive heat stress worse than *ever* imagined! McClure's mental discipline and stamina proved to be important qualities in an astronaut.

Although the Manhigh program soon ended, Colonel Stapp had plans for another high-altitude mission. This time, he planned for a pilot to *bail out* from the edge of space!

FREE FALL: PROJECT EXCELSIOR

In thinking about the future of space travel, Colonel Stapp knew that an astronaut would need to get outside his vehicle either to repair it or to bail out back to Earth in case of emergency. Led by Captain Joe Kittinger, Project Excelsior set out to discover how a person might survive such a *life-threatening* ordeal!

Kittinger proposed that a pilot travel 100,000 miles above the surface of the earth in an open gondola — and then *jump out*! The secret was free-falling to an altitude where the opening shock of the parachute wouldn't be *fatal*.

SPIN TEST DUMMIES!

Tests with dummies found that drops from more than 100,000 feet resulted in a violent spinning motion. In fact, the spinning was *so* fast it could kill a man!

An air force engineer named Francis Beaupre came up with a brand-new parachute design that could help a person land as quickly as possible. Two different chutes would open, stabilizing the parachutist.

KITTINGER'S FALL

On November 16, 1959, after the crew had gone over a thousand-item checklist, Captain Kittinger was ready to go. The balloon rose, the pressure suit inflated, and everything seemed normal.

But at 76,000 feet, just as he prepared to jump, Kittinger discovered he was *trapped* in his seat. Finally, he wrenched himself free — but set off the parachute release

CONFIDENTIAL FILES!

Project Manhigh gave NASA their research for designing pressure suits and space capsules. These materials would be used by NASA for *years* afterward!

CONFIDENTIAL FILES!

The Project Manhigh and Project Excelsior programs paved the way for humankind's great space voyages. The American programs that followed these early attempts at space flight were Project Mercury, Project Gemini, and, finally, the Project Apollo moon program. On July 20, 1969, Neil Armstrong and Edwin Aldrin of *Apollo 11* became the first humans to walk on the moon!

timer. Instead of falling a full sixteen seconds, he fell just *two* seconds before the second parachute released.

The chute wrapped around Kittinger's neck and he went into a flat spin. But thanks to Beaupre's parachute design, the extra lines broke away. Kittinger miraculously survived the spin and landed safely.

EXCELSIOR II AND III

Although he was nearly killed, Kittinger wanted to try to free-fall again. A month later, he jumped from 74,700 feet and landed perfectly! Finally, he was ready for the final feat — a jump from 100,000 feet above Earth.

The balloon for Excelsior III rose without incident. But at 40,000 feet, Kittinger discovered the pressure suit glove on his right hand wasn't working. That meant that his hand would feel unbearably cold and swell to twice its normal size — but it wouldn't kill him.

Kittinger decided not to mention the glove to the crew. And when he reached 100,000 feet, he leaped off the highest step in the world. Kittinger fell at a speed of 714 miles per hour, the first man to go *supersonic* without an airplane!

TEST YOUR SECRET INTELLIGENCE!

Although other programs competed for government funding for the space race, NASA, with rocket power, won the entire $100 million space budget! True or false?

(Answer: True)

SUCCESS!

After a day, Kittinger's hand returned to normal. Best of all, the Excelsior III team had proved their goal: They learned that future space travelers could bail out from 100,000 feet — *and survive*.

Although this was the last mission for the Manhigh team, the brave pre-astronauts gathered information still used in the space program today. Their imagination and courage pulled America into the space race, leading the way for humankind's greatest journeys into uncharted territories.

Photodisc

5

PSYCHIC SPIES

More than fifty years ago, a new kind of spy burst onto the international espionage scene. Without ever leaving their own countries, psychic spies could discover secrets around the world – simply by using the incredible power of the human mind!

PSYCHOLOGICAL ESPIONAGE!

Can some people really "read minds"? Are there some gifted individuals who can use their minds to "travel" thousands of miles — and actually *infiltrate* enemy territory? For years, the CIA (Central Intelligence Agency) and other government agencies around the world secretly used psychic spying to defend their countries.

Did it *really* work? Read about some of the most famous psychic spying cases and decide for yourself!

PRECOGNITION

Remember the movie *The Sixth Sense*, in which a young boy could see dead people? Another kind of "sixth sense" is precognition, the ability that enables a person to envision events — *before* they happen! The feeling that something is going to happen is called a premonition.

In 1987, Captain Paul H. Smith was working with STARGATE, a special program that used psychic spying techniques and worked closely with many branches of the U.S. government. One day, Smith envisioned smoke, fire, people screaming, and a metal structure in water. Within hours, an Iraqi fighter jet mistakenly fired at a U.S. ship — and tragically, thirty-seven Americans were killed! It seems Captain Smith had used the power of precognition to predict this horrible event. But unfortunately, he was unable to prevent it from happening! Still, his amazing feat showed the power of the mind.

MODERN DOWSING

Dowsing is the ancient art of using a divining rod — a special stick — to find water. Ancients believed that, when used by a psychic, the rod would start to tremble and point to ground where water could be found.

In a similar way, psychic spies used "map

dowsing" to pinpoint possible targets around the world! The psychic spy would hold a piece of string over a map and picture a specific object. Once located, the string would swing toward the target's coordinates on the map!

Agents in Vietnam during the Vietnam War used map dowsing techniques to find hidden tunnels. And in 1978, psychic spies used the method to find a plane that had crashed in Africa!

?

TEST YOUR SECRET INTELLIGENCE!

**Experts believe that psychic ability is a natural talent, like a talent for music or art, and can be developed through practice.
True or false?**

(Answer: True)

ESP AND REMOTE VIEWING

In the 1930s, scientists at Duke University in North Carolina came up with the term *extrasensory perception*, or ESP, to describe the ability to "see" into the next room — or even around the world — by simply concentrating! Now called remote viewing, that amazing ability has secretly been used by spies *for years*.

According to scientists, remote viewing works best when people have few distractions. By sitting in a room painted all one color and shielded from sound and light, people with psychic abilities can "travel" through their minds to other locations. There, they poke around to "find" classified information! Sounds pretty cool, right?

Remote viewing became one of the most-used forms of psychic spying, especially during the period of time after World War II known as the Cold War.

THE COLD WAR: A TIME OF SPIES

In the years following the end of World War II, in 1945, political differences between the United States and the Soviet Union grew. The United States felt that its strong principles of democracy conflicted with the Soviet Union's belief in the Communist system. By 1947, the United States and the Soviet Union were engaged in a Cold War, in which they used every method short  of direct military battles to defeat the enemy government. The struggle against the threat of Communism would last for more than forty years.

The Cold War was not a land war, in which soldiers march in to take over another country.

Instead, it was a way to defend democracy in the United States and in other countries around the world from the possible threat of Communism. Gathering information — often through the use of spies — was an important part of the U.S. defense strategy.

Because of this, the Cold War was one of the most important times for spies, especially *psychic spies*, in the history of our country!

A PSYCHIC "WAR"?

In the 1950s, the CIA created a secret program that would use psychological warfare, such as remote viewing, hypnosis, and other methods of mind control. Named MK-Ultra, the program was experimental at first. But by 1960, a strange international episode set the stage for a full-blown psychic espionage face-off between the United States and the Soviet Union!

It all began when an article in a French scientific journal claimed that a Maryland psychic had *telepathically* sent information to the U.S.S. *Nautilus*, a submarine beneath the Arctic Ocean, in 1959. Telepathic communication means that

CONFIDENTIAL

CONFIDENTIAL FILES!

Remote viewing allows psychics to *see* things that other people cannot see. But remote viewing isn't just limited to sight. Those who have the remote viewing ability say that information comes through to them as smells, sounds, feelings, and even *tastes*!

one person just *thinks of* something — and another person receives the message!

News of the top secret experiment spread quickly around the world. Even though the whole thing may have been a hoax, both the United States and the Soviet Union began competing to develop psychic spying strategies!

SECRET WEAPONS

By the late 1960s, intelligence reports claimed the Soviets were using *psychic weapons* against Americans in Moscow! At that time, several American diplomats living in the Soviet Union's capital suddenly became seriously ill. The diplomats returned to the United States, were diagnosed with cancer, and died soon after. And in 1972, other American diplomats visiting Moscow with President Richard Nixon also suddenly got very sick! Was it simply a coincidence . . . or something more sinister?

Experts now believe other factors may have caused the illness. But at the time, the push was on to pump up U.S. research into the paranormal — and to develop psychic weaponry to fight the Soviets!

INCREDIBLE VISIONS IN CALIFORNIA

One of the first steps in using psychic espionage to fight the Soviet Union was the founding of a lab in California that specialized in top secret experiments. By the early 1970s, the Stanford Research Institute (SRI) in Palo Alto, California, became the most important center for psychic spy research in the country. Collaborations between scientist Dr. Harold Puthoff and gifted psychics resulted in incredible information-gathering missions.

TEST YOUR SECRET INTELLIGENCE!

For decades, Russians were fascinated with ESP, mind control, and precognition. But when Joseph Stalin came to power in 1928, all paranormal activity was "officially" outlawed! True or false?

(Answer: True)

64

AMAZING PSYCHICS

To test psychic ability, Dr. Puthoff asked people to describe an object hidden inside a box. One day, a New York psychic named Ingo Swann came in and said, "This is trivial. . . . I can see anywhere on the planet." Naturally, Dr. Puthoff was skeptical! (Wouldn't *you* be?)

CONFIDENTIAL FILES!

The remote viewing results at SRI were so accurate sometimes that the CIA didn't even want to believe them! But after many investigations, the agency decided that psychic searches were real — and could be useful for spying on enemies of the United States!

But as Dr. Puthoff tested Swann, he discovered Swann could really "see" psychically into other places! The CIA heard about the tests and awarded the Stanford Research Institute a contract to explore whether psychics could be used for espionage!

Soon a talented psychic named Pat Price joined the experiments at the SRI. The results would prove to be *astounding.* . . .

SECRET CODES

In a 1974 experiment, Swann and Price set out

to use remote viewing to see the weekend home of a CIA agent. And they wound up discovering a secret National Security Administration (NSA) facility instead!

Both men "entered" the facility through remote viewing. Pat Price was even able to "look" through a file with secret code names.

The facility was *so* top secret, even the CIA didn't know about it! But when the CIA looked into it, they discovered it was real. And the files were just as Price had described them. So it seemed psychics could be useful after all!

TEST YOUR SECRET INTELLIGENCE!

The CIA was so skeptical of psychic Pat Price that they refused an offer to have him work for them. True or False?

(Answer: False. The CIA was so impressed by Price's psychic powers that they asked him to work for the agency!)

MISSION: BREAK-IN!

In 1949, the Soviet Union's Semipalatinsk facility was used for the first Soviet atomic bomb test. In 1974, Pat Price remotely viewed and sketched the facility. The CIA was impressed when spy satellites confirmed the accuracy of his drawings, proving that psychic espionage could really work!

The CIA asked Price to target the country Libya, which was backed by the Soviets. Price psychically found secret training centers for guerrilla fighters! Photos later confirmed Price's reports were true.

STARGATE

The CIA eventually gave up control over psychic espionage projects. But starting in 1975, the government began sponsoring psychic investigations through the little-known Defense Intelligence Agency, or DIA. Over the next twenty years, the DIA used several top secret code names, such as Grill Flame, Sun Streak, and SCANATE. Today, STARGATE is the name most associated with America's psychic espionage adventures!

SECRET TRAINING

STARGATE was a full-time unit on call at all times for *all* government agencies that required psychic services. The program participated in every major American engagement throughout the world from the 1970s through the 1990s. It also worked to protect America from the psychic espionage of *other* nations.

STARGATE secretly recruited and trained psychics from all branches of the military. If a recruit was a natural leader, confident, and artistically inclined, he or she was considered a good candidate. In 1977, Vietnam War veteran Joe McMoneagle was chosen to become a STARGATE psychic spy — and he turned out to be one of the most talented remote viewers *ever!*

A PSYCHIC STAR

When Joe McMoneagle was asked to find a CIA agent in an unknown location in the United States, he drew detailed pictures of windmills. It turned out the agent was hiding out near a windmill farm in California!

McMoneagle worked on dozens of missions. His psychic work took him everywhere — from searching for hostages in the Iranian city of Teheran to discovering a new kind of submarine in a shipyard in Siberia. His intelligence work uncovered information that had never even been *considered* before!

In 1981, Joe McMoneagle's psychic ability was put to the ultimate test. His mission? To search the world for a missing NATO (North Atlantic Treaty Organization) officer!

SEEKING GENERAL DOZIER

When General James Dozier was kidnapped by a terrorist group in Italy, Joe McMoneagle was called in to help. Working from Fort Meade, Maryland, McMoneagle described and sketched a detailed picture of a city on the coast. He sensed the city was called "Padova" or "Padua."

"Padova" is in fact the Italian name for "Padua," a city in Italy. McMoneagle had found the exact city — Padua, Italy — where General Dozier was held captive. Later, counterterrorist troops found and rescued the general. This incident proved that psychics could not only be useful . . . they could be heroes!

TEST YOUR SECRET INTELLIGENCE!

If you have the gift of remote viewing, you can go on vacation — to any destination you choose — for weeks at a time through your mind! True or false?

(Answer: False. Nobody can sustain uninterrupted weeks of remote viewing!)

PSYCHIC SPIES TODAY

What are psychic spies doing *now*? After the Cold War ended, Congress decided to officially shut down psychic espionage programs in the United States. But many experts agree that when the need arises, U.S. intelligence agencies may *still* call upon a secret corps of psychic spies to venture into the unknown. . . .

TOP SECRET: THE ULTIMATE CHALLENGE!

You've traveled through time, across oceans, and even into space to explore some of the world's most amazing secrets. Now, take the ultimate challenge . . . and see how much you remember about undercover history!

1. **Ace pilot Jerrie Cobb began flying at the age of:**
   a. 12
   b. 13
   c. 14

2. **Who was the first man to survive 24 hours on the edge of space?**
   a. David Simons
   b. Mr. Manhigh
   c. Dr. Stapp

3. **What was the name of the program for government agencies that required psychic services?**
   a. SUNSEARCH
   b. WINDGATE
   c. STARGATE

4. **Auguste Piccard invented the first:**
   a. bathyscaphe
   b. bathysphere
   c. bathyslide

5. **Captain Joe Kittinger made history by free-falling the farthest distance *ever* above Earth. He jumped from:**
   a. 100,000 feet
   b. 200,000 feet
   c. 10,000 feet

6. **In 1940, Jackie Cochran set a new speed record for flying that was faster than any woman *or man* had ever flown before! That speed was:**
   a. 447 miles per hour
   b. 332 miles per hour
   c. 748 miles per hour

7. **The Challenger Deep lies off the coast of which island?**
   a. Tahiti
   b. Puerto Rico
   c. Guam

8. **What does DIA stand for?**
   a. Defense Intelligence Agency
   b. Defensive International Association
   c. Dense Intellectual Agency

9. **Which of the following brave people is honored at Yad Vashem?**
   a. Joe McMoneagle
   b. Aristides de Sousa Mendes
   c. Amelia Earhart

10. **What did Varian Fry call Harry Bingham when he signed his book?**
    a. his best friend
    b. his worst enemy
    c. his partner in crime

UNDERCOVER GLOSSARY

Attaché (A-tah-shay): a member of a diplomatic staff for another country.

Battering ram (BAT-a-ring RAM): a military engine consisting of a large wooden beam with a head of iron.

Conspiracy (con-SPIR-a-see): the act of planning and acting together secretly, possibly for a danger-ous or unlawful goal.

Diplomat (DIP-loh-mat): a person whose job it is to maintain working relation-ships between nations.

Fathom (FA-thum): a mea-sure of length of about six feet, used mainly in measur-ing the depth of water.

Forklift (FORK-lift): a self-propelled machine for lifting and transporting heavy objects.

G force (GEE FORS) (*Gravity force*): the force of gravity during acceleration or deceleration.

Gasket sealant (GAS-ket SEEL-ant): a substance used to seal a surface to prevent leakage of a liq-uid or gas.

Gondola (GON-doh-la): an airtight enclosure sus-pended from a balloon for carrying passengers or instruments.

CONFIDENTIAL

Guerrilla (guh-ril-a) fighters: an independent band of fighters not belonging to a government military.

Laundering (LAWN-der-ing): transferring illegally obtained money through an outside person or country in order to conceal the true source.

Paranormal (PAH-rah-NOR-mal): beyond the normal; something that cannot be explained scientifically or through ordinary knowledge.

Refugee (ref-you-GEE): one who flees, usually to a foreign country, to escape danger or persecution.

Stratosphere (STRA-tos-feer): the upper part of the earth's atmosphere.

Telepathy (ta-LEH-pah-thee): communication between two or more minds; transference of thought.

Typhoon (TIE-foon): a tropical windstorm that occurs in the western Pacific or Indian Oceans.